Barrage™
VOLUME 2

Sheet music for the intermediate to advanced violinist

The Barrage Book – Volume 2

International Standard Music Number
M-706020-09-9

CM – 2

Swath Publishing
23 Taylor Bay
Calgary, Alberta, Canada
T3L 2P6
Ph: (403) 208-4040
Fx: (403) 208-4042
Web: www.barrage.org

Cover artwork by Xentel DM Inc.

SWATH PUBLISHING   MEL BAY®

1 2 3 4 5 6 7 8 9 0

Contents

Dean Marshall

Over the past decade, Dean Marshall has distinguished himself as a versatile pedagogue, composer, arranger and performer. As the current Artistic Director of the hot new fiddle group BARRAGE and as the past Artistic Director of the Calgary Fiddlers Association and the Fiddlers GF, Mr. Marshall has stretched the parameters of violin playing by incorporating fiddling and traditional music styles with a contemporary worldbeat sound. He has also produced numerous recording and video projects.

Mr. Marshall's unique and highly effective approach to pedagogy ensures that he is in great demand as a teacher. His success in developing string players at all levels has resulted in workshops and lectures at the Midwest International Orchestra and Band Workshop, European String Teachers Association, Hawaii Suzuki Institute, Ohio Music Educators Conference and the International String Workshops. His composing and arranging credits include writing and producing the highly successful "Fiddle Club" series published by Swath Publishing. He has also served as composer and arranger for Richard Hayman and the Calgary Philharmonic Orchestra.

Trained as a classical violinist, Mr. Marshall is a graduate of the University of Toronto and Mount Royal College Conservatory. In addition to touring England, Scotland, Australia, the USA and Japan as a performer he is also a former winner of first prize in the Grand North American Fiddle Championships.

Barrage

This hot young troupe of seven violinists, one percussionist, one kit player, guitarist, bass and keyboard players, perform a mix of original worldbeat music by Dean Marshall, with infectious and irresistible energy. BARRAGE combines jazz, swing, celtic roots, rock, klezmer, country, calypso and every musical style in-between to create an eclectic and electrifying assault on the senses.

Since its creation in 1996 by John Crozman, Dean Marshall, Anthony Moore, Jana Wyber and Larry Saloff, BARRAGE has traveled the world, delighting audiences and critics alike. The show takes a new-fashioned look at musical traditions in an exciting, innovative theatrical evening that highlights the performers' amazing versatility and virtuosity. Composer Dean Marshall blends styles from all over the world in an effortless, fun and energetic way. This totally original and refreshing approach is a unique blend of entertainment that breaks down stylistic barriers and, consequently, appeals to all ages. As a group, these young performers amaze with their unstoppable vivacity; individually they cite influences from Mozart to Charlie Daniels!

Preface

I cannot tell you how excited I am to get this music out to you! We have had literally hundreds and hundreds of requests for the music of BARRAGE! The problem in producing this publication lay in the intricacy of the part writing and the complexity of the arranging. The full score was far too thick musically to be performed by a single violin player, and far too technically demanding for a large-scale fiddle group. My challenge was to simplify and change the 7-violin part writing to 1 and 3-violin part writing. This publication is the result of this process. I have included various markings (bar numbers, fingerings, and bowings), which I have found especially helpful in group situations. As always, experienced players may want to alter some of these markings and add their own to reflect their personal style. In terms of difficulty level, these arrangements are definitely written for the more intermediate to advanced player.

As most of the tunes are intended for group performance, there are many sections in the music marked 'tutti'. Unless otherwise indicated, the solo parts should play in all tutti sections. In addition, for solo, duet, and trio sections, the number given first refers to the part carrying the melody.

All the tunes in the book have been recorded by BARRAGE and are available on CD. You will also find that most of the tunes are available on video and DVD.

For those individuals and groups that would like to perform this music, piano (bass) and guitar accompaniments are available that compliment this book.

I would like to thank Rodd Bauman for his tireless effort in editing and proofreading this book.

I hope that this material will serve as a valuable resource for anyone interested in the music of BARRAGE.

Sincerely,

Dean Marshall

Dean Marshall

Violin I

What's Going On?

by Dean Marshall

Optional: Drum (Bodhran) - play constant eigth note pulse

4

Violin I

6

Violin I

8

Violin 2 Solo

Gradually move closer to the bridge (Ponticello)

Violin 2

What's Going On?

by Dean Marshall

Optional: Drum (Bodhran) - play constant eigth note pulse

Violin 2

Violin 2

14

Violin 2

15

Violin 3

What's Going On?

by Dean Marshall

Optional: Drum (Bodhran) - play constant eigth note pulse

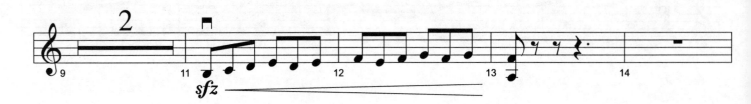

16

Violin 3

Violin 3

Violin I

Texas Swing

by Dean Marshall

Violin I

24

Violin I

26

Violin I

27

Violin 2

Texas Swing

by Dean Marshall

29

Violin 2

30

31

Violin 2

Violin I

Calypso Jam

by Dean Marshall

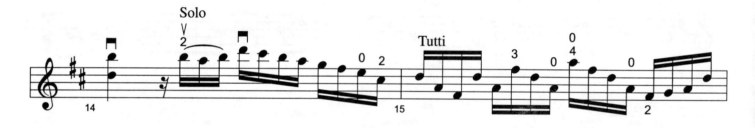

34

Violin I

Violin 1 & 2 (or 1 & 3) Duet

Violin I

37

Violin 2

Calypso Jam

by Dean Marshall

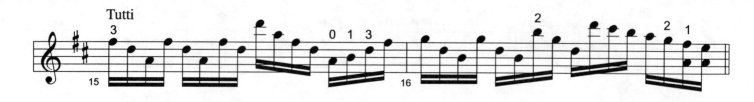

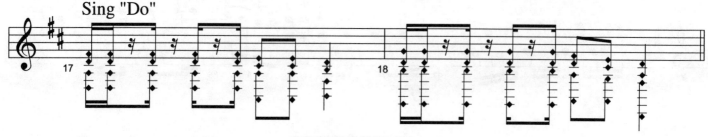

Violin 2

Violins answer

Sing "Do"

Violins answer

Violin 2 & 3 Duet with Violin 1 strumming

Play on violin or "D" whistle

Violin 2

Violin 2

41

Violin 2

42

Calypso Jam

Violin 3

by Dean Marshall

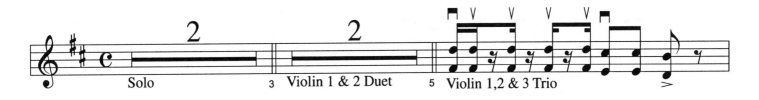

Solo   Violin 1 & 2 Duet   Violin 1,2 & 3 Trio

sim.

Solo   Tutti

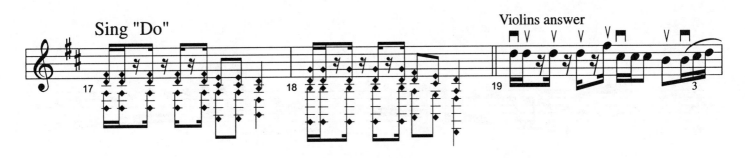

Sing "Do"   Violins answer

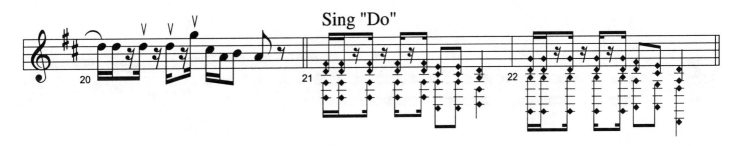

Sing "Do"

Violin 3

Violins answer

Violin 2 & 3 Duet
with Violin 1 strumming

Play on violin or "D" whistle

Violin 3

Violin I

Until We Meet Again

by R.A. Zimmer
arranged by Dean Marshall

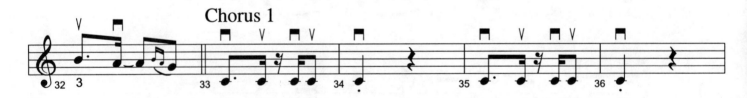

Fiddle Theme 1 (Violin 2 Solo)

Verse 2

Chorus 2

Violin I

Fiddle Theme 2 (Violin 2 Solo)

Violin 1 Solo

Bridge

Verse 3

Chorus 3

Coda Violin 1 Solo

Violin 1 Solo Ends Violin 2 Solo

Violin 2 Solo ends

Until We Meet Again

Violin 2

by R.A. Zimmer
arranged by Dean Marshall

Fiddle Theme 1 (Violin 2 Solo)

Fiddle Themes 1 & 2 may be played on an "F" tin whistle (octave higher)

Verse 2

Chorus 2

Violin 2

54

Until We Meet Again

Violin 3

by R.A. Zimmer
arranged by Dean Marshall

Fiddle Theme 1 (Violin 2 Solo)

Verse 2

Chorus 2

Violin 3

Chorus 3

Coda

Violin 1 Solo

Violin 1 Solo Ends

Violin 2 Solo

Violin 2 Solo ends

cresc.

f

ff decresc.

Vocal

Until We Meet Again

by R.A. Zimmer
arranged by Dean Marshall

Verse 1

May the road

rise up to me-et you _____ May the wind be

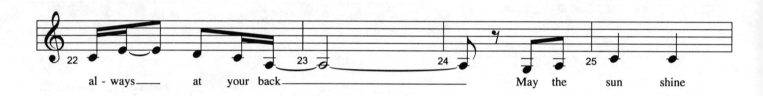

al-ways ___ at your back _____ May the sun shine

warm u-pon ___ your face ___ now _____ May the rains fall

Chorus 1

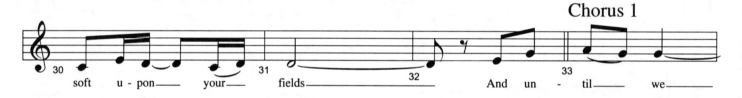

soft u-pon ___ your ___ fields _____ And un-til ___ we ___

meet a-gain _____ And un-til ___ we ___ meet a-gain ___

_____ May ___ God hold ___ you in the palm ___ of His ___

Hand May ___ God hold ___ you in the palm ___ of His ___

Vocal

May the road rise up to meet you
May the wind be at your back
May the sun shine warm upon your face May the
rain fall soft upon your fields. May this

Verse 3

world and all its won - ders. Be a home to
all hu - ma - ni - ty May the peo ple
find a com - mon pur - pose. May we help one a -

Chorus 3

no - ther to sur - vive. And un - til we

Vocal

Seven Wicked Reels

Reel 7

by Dean Marshall

Reel 5

Reel 3

69

Reel I

Other Publications from SWATH

The Fiddle Club Volumes 1-3
Arranged and Composed by Dean Marshall
In three graded volumes, The Fiddle Club is an excellent way for the avid violinist to learn the fiddle style. Each volume comes with separate violin book, piano/guitar accompaniment book, and compact disc recording (each sold separately). Each volume of The Fiddle Club contains arrangements of tunes for one to three fiddles, making it appropriate for individual or group study.

The Barrage Book Volume 1-2
By Dean Marshall
Containing sheet music for many of the tunes played by the internationally acclaimed group BARRAGE, The Barrage Books Volume 1 & 2 are guaranteed to inspire the serious violin student. All arrangements can be played as solo pieces, though most of the tunes have been arranged for three or more violins. All pieces in The Barrage Books have been recorded, and can be heard on the commercial recordings 'Barrage – Live in Europe', and 'Barrage'.

Products Under Development

The Fiddle Club Volume 4
By Dean Marshall
The introduction to The Fiddle Club - The Fiddle Club Volume 4 is intended for the beginning violinist. Piano/guitar accompaniments will also be available.

Mountain Spring - string orchestra arrangement
Written by Dean Marshall
Frequently requested and performed worldwide by Barrage, Mountain Spring is a beautiful and moving ballad. Intermediate level string orchestra.

Calypso Jam - string orchestra arrangement
Written by Dean Marshall
Frequently requested and performed worldwide by Barrage, Calypso Jam is an energetic and exciting piece. Intermediate level string orchestra.

Folk Tunes for Flute
By Dean Marshall
Edited and Arranged by Ingrid Crozman
A new addition to our catalog, Folk Tunes for Flute is an excellent way to spark the interest of any flute student. In arrangements for one, two, and three flutes, this compilation introduces the flute player to traditional folk music in a creative and innovative way. Piano/guitar accompaniments will also be available.

Notes